WICCA

ALTAR AND TOOLS

A Beginner's Guide to Wiccan Altars, Tools for Spellwork, and Casting the Circle

LISA CHAMBERLAIN

Wicca Altar and Tools

Copyright © 2015 by Lisa Chamberlain.

All rights reserved. No part of this book may be reproduced in any form without permission in writing from the author. Reviewers may quote brief passages in reviews

Published by **Chamberlain Publications (Wicca Shorts)**

ISBN: 151760866X

ISBN-13: 978-1517608668

Disclaimer

No part of this publication may be reproduced or transmitted in any form or by any means, mechanical or electronic, including photocopying or recording, or by any information storage and retrieval system, or transmitted by email without permission in writing from the publisher.

While all attempts have been made to verify the information provided in this publication, neither the author nor the publisher assumes any responsibility for errors, omissions, or contrary interpretations of the subject matter herein.

This book is for entertainment purposes only. The views expressed are those of the author alone, and should not be taken as expert instruction or commands. The reader is responsible for his or her own actions.

Adherence to all applicable laws and regulations, including international, federal, state, and local governing professional licensing, business practices, advertising, and all other aspects of doing business in the US, Canada, or any other jurisdiction is the sole responsibility of the purchaser or reader.

Neither the author nor the publisher assumes any responsibility or liability whatsoever on the behalf of the purchaser or reader of these materials.

Any perceived slight of any individual or organization is purely unintentional.

YOUR FREE GIFT

Thank you for adding this book to your Wiccan library! To learn more, why not join Lisa's Wiccan community and get an exclusive, free spell book?

The book is a great starting point for anyone looking to try their hand at practicing magic. The ten beginner-friendly spells can help you to create a positive atmosphere within your home, protect yourself from negativity, and attract love, health, and prosperity.

Little Book of Spells is now available to read on your laptop, phone, tablet, Kindle or Nook device!

To download, simply visit the following link:

www.wiccaliving.com/bonus

GET THREE FREE AUDIOBOOKS FROM LISA CHAMBERLAIN

Did you know that all of Lisa's books are available in audiobook format? Best of all, you can get **three audiobooks completely free** as part of a 30-day trial with Audible.

Wicca Starter Kit contains three of Lisa's most popular books for beginning Wiccans, all in one convenient place. It's the best and easiest way to learn more about Wicca while also taking audiobooks for a spin! Simply visit:

www.wiccaliving.com/free-wiccan-audiobooks

Alternatively, *Spellbook Starter Kit* is the ideal option for building your magical repertoire using candle and color magic, crystals and mineral stones, and magical herbs. Three spellbooks —over 150 spells—are available in one free volume, here:

www.wiccaliving.com/free-spell-audiobooks

Audible members receive free audiobooks every month, as well as exclusive discounts. It's a great way to experiment and see if audiobook learning works for you.

If you're not satisfied, you can cancel anytime within the trial period. You won't be charged, and you can still keep your books!

CONTENTS

Introduction 10

Part One: The Wicca Altar 14

  The Altar: A Universal Means of Worship 15
  The Use of the Altar in Wicca... 19
    Origins of the Wicca Altar 20
    Common "Tools" and their Arrangements 21
    Aligning Energies 22
    Creating an Altar of Your Own 24
  The Altar and the Circle.. 27
    Placing the Altar... 31
    Setting Up Your Altar... 32

Part Two: The Tools of Wiccan Ritual and Magic 35

  The Basics 36
    Altar Cloth 36
    Altar Candles 37
    Deity Representations 38
    Athame... 39
    Wand 40
    Chalice 42
    Cakes and Plates.. 43
    Incense (Air Representation)... 44
    Candle (Fire Representation).. 47
    Dish of Water (Water Representation) 48

- *Dish of Sea Salt or Soil (Earth Representation)* 49
- *Anointing Oils* 50
- *Your Book of Shadows* 51
- Further Options 53
  - *Broom* 53
  - *A Witch's Bell/Devil Driver* 55
  - *A Pentacle Slab* 56
  - *Incense Accessories* 57
  - *Cauldron* 59
  - *Candle Snuffer* 60
  - *Long Matches or Barbecue Lighter* 61
  - *Writing Utensil (Pen or Pencil)* 61
  - *Baskets* 62
  - *Bucket of Water* 62
  - *Next Steps* 62
- Ritual Wear 64
  - *Pentacle* 65
  - *Gemstone Jewelry* 66
  - *Jewelry with Sigils* 68
  - *Ritual Robes* 68
  - *Cloaks* 69
- Tools and Ingredients for Spellwork 71
  - *Parchment* 72
  - *Boline* 73
  - *Candles* 73
  - *Crystals and Other Mineral Stones* 74
  - *Incense, Dried Herbs, and Essential Oils* 75
  - *Magic Cord and Ribbon* 75
  - *Divination Tools* 76
  - *A Hand Drum or Rhythmic Music* 76
  - *Mortar and Pestle* 77

Empty Bottles and Jars 77
Multi-Tab Notebooks 78
Different Colors of Journals 79
Fabrics and Sewing Materials 79

Part Three: Finding, Purchasing, and Preparing Your Tools 81

Buying and Purchasing Wicca Tools 82
Purchasing Supplies in Person 83
Purchasing Supplies Online 84
Consider the Item's Origins 86
Affordable or Extravagant? 88
Ways to Save Money for Rituals and Spellwork 89
Clearing and Consecrating Your Tools for Ritual and Spellwork 93
A Clearing and Consecration Ritual 95
When to Perform the Rites on Your Items 99

Conclusion 101

Suggestions for Further Reading 104
Three Free Audiobooks Promotion 105
More Books by Lisa Chamberlain 106
Free Gift Reminder 108

INTRODUCTION

Welcome to this beginner's guide to the Wiccan altar and the tools of the Craft.

Whether you're just exploring your curiosity about this fairly unusual religion, or whether you've decided you're definitely ready to wade further into the waters of Wiccan wisdom, you'll find solid information and practical advice in these pages.

You most likely already know that Wicca is very different from most other contemporary religions.

There is no single holy text to follow, no one, all-encompassing deity, and there are no official buildings—churches, temples, or otherwise—where worship and prayer take place.

There are also no specific centuries-old traditions to follow, since Wicca is a modern religion inspired by—but not beholden to—practices from earlier times in history.

There are a few basic tenets—such as honoring and respecting Nature and refraining from doing harm to others—and a general template of ritual activity that hold practitioners under the umbrella title of "Wicca," but in reality, traditions and practices are extremely widely varied, from continent to continent, coven to coven, and, of course, individual to individual.

Nonetheless, Wicca still shares one significant element with various other religions around the globe: the use of an altar and of other specific objects to honor and communicate with the divine.

Just like Christians, Buddhists and Hindus, Wiccans make use of a physical place in order to practice their faith. And like Buddhist statues or Catholic rosaries, the tools of Wicca serve to focus the intentional energy of the practitioner in worship. Through symbolism and ritual, the tools—as well as the altar itself—connect us with the Goddess and the God in celebration of our participation in the natural cycles of life on Earth.

While in other religions, the altar may or may not feature prominently in one's daily practice of faith, the altar is widely considered to be the central physical focus of Wiccan spiritual activity. The altar hosts the rituals for Sabbats and Esbats, and is usually the place where spellwork happens (for those Wiccans who practice magic).

It is the most important place of power in the Wiccan faith. For those wishing to enter Wicca, acquiring or creating a personal altar is an excellent place to begin.

This guide provides an introduction to the Wiccan altar, as well as its spiritual and magical tools.

It begins with a brief overview of the use of religious altars around the globe and throughout time, before moving into a closer look at the origins and history of the altar as it's known to Wiccans. You'll also find ideas for acquiring or "repurposing" your own altar, if you don't have one already.

Then, we'll cover the basic, most commonly used ritual tools traditionally found in most branches of Wicca, keeping in mind, of course, that actual practices vary widely.

Next, for those interested in deepening their Wiccan experience through the practice of magic, we'll cover the most widely employed "ingredients" used in Wiccan spellwork.

Finally, you'll find suggestions for locating and buying (or otherwise acquiring) tools for ritual and spellwork, and instructions for energetic clearing and charging—a very important step.

Because Wicca is such a diverse set of beliefs and practices, it's important to acknowledge that some who identify as Wiccans do not practice magic, and that magic is certainly not a requirement!

However, many Wiccans do, and this may be the element that most draws newcomers to the faith. In fact, it's the spellwork itself that some argue truly sets Wicca apart from other, more "contemplative" religions.

Rather than simply praying, showing gratitude, and then hoping for one's prayers to come true, Wiccans actively participate in the shaping of the events in their lives.

Using our tools at the altar, we center, focus, and strengthen the energy and power that are a natural result of communication and solidarity with the forces of Nature and the oneness of the Universe.

With that belief in mind, this guide treats the tools of ritual and the tools of spellcraft as equally powerful and worthy of respect.

It's recommended that you read widely about Wicca, as no single source can ever possibly tell you everything you need to know.

Nonetheless, if you follow this guide, you will find yourself well-prepared for beginning your own practice of observing the Sabbats and Esbats, working spells, and performing other various rites and rituals that make up the wonderfully eclectic faith we call Wicca.

Blessed Be.

PART ONE
THE WICCA ALTAR

THE ALTAR: A UNIVERSAL MEANS OF WORSHIP

Assuming that you come from a place where Western beliefs are prevalent, you're probably already aware of what an altar is.

Christianity makes the most prevalent use of altars in contemporary organized religion, but the altar is also found in many Eastern spiritual traditions, including Buddhism, Taoism, Hinduism, and Shinto.

An altar is generally defined as a structure on which offerings are made to one or more deities, but it can also be a place where ancestors are honored or treasured objects with spiritual significance are kept.

Altars can be found within shrines and temples, and also in people's homes. (Some people think of "shrines" and "altars" as being essentially the same thing.)

Essentially, most cultures throughout history have, at some point or other, employed the use of an altar for the purposes of worship, prayer, and, yes, even spell-casting.

It might surprise followers of Christianity to realize that the altar itself has its roots in pre-Judaic "pagan" traditions. It was the work of the earliest Jews to eradicate competition between their "God" and the "other gods" mentioned in the Old Testament.

It's possible that the use of the altar was adapted from those earlier spiritual traditions, since we find the practice so widespread among other religions that date even further back than the first records of Judaic worship.

The first altar mentioned in the Hebrew Bible was built by Noah, the central figure of the Hebrew version of the myth of the Great Flood.

The altar in ancient Judaism was used for offering sacrifices to the Jewish God, though this practice changed over time for various reasons.

Christianity's use of the altar was adapted, of course, from Judaism, but it evolved into a place for honoring the sacrifice of the life of Jesus through symbolic re-creation.

In terms of what would now be considered the "Pagan" history of altars, we see evidence in the ancient cultures of Greece, Rome, Norway, Egypt, Ireland, and the Ottoman Empire, where altars were used to venerate deities, leave offerings, make sacrifices, and send prayers. It's generally from these locations—and particularly those in what we consider to be the "Western" world—that Wicca draws its inspiration.

If we had some way of going back in time, we might find that altars existed even in the earliest days of human activity, when the fire would have been given glory. Considering that this was the most impressive discovery made by man next to the wheel, it wouldn't be that far-fetched to imagine our most ancient ancestors dancing around the fire after a big catch and the resulting feast, raising the energy and rejoicing in the night.

We can't possibly know what an altar would have looked like back then, but we can safely assume that people would have used what they had, which would mean materials that are still utilized to this day: stone, wood, a slab of granite. An altar may have even been nothing more than an unraveled cloth, or even a designated patch of the ground beneath one's feet.

Altars are indeed found all over the globe, in many different forms and for fairly widely varying purposes from tradition to tradition.

However, an altar is not strictly necessary for spiritual communion with the divine. In many religious traditions, the human body is considered to be the principal "temple" of worship.

As such, we can imagine ourselves to be places of worship for the divine. The altar is really a physical extension of the manifestation of our own divinity, and from a Wiccan perspective, a place to focus the connection between our personal energy and that of Akasha, or "spirit."

THE USE OF THE ALTAR IN WICCA

As with any other religion or spiritual tradition, the altar in Wicca is a place to both worship and connect with the divine.

However, unlike most other religions, Wicca provides an avenue for a very direct kind of participation—what we might actually call "co-creation" with the forces of the Universe that shape our daily lives.

Through meditation, energy raising, prayer, and/or spellwork, Wiccans work actively to improve the state of things in their personal spheres as well as in the world at large.

The altar serves as the physical focal point for this work.

It is used most commonly for ritual celebrations at the eight Sabbats and thirteen Esbats (Full Moons) on the Wheel of the Year, but can really be used at any time—

for spellwork, or just for quiet contemplation or meditation.

ORIGINS OF THE WICCA ALTAR

The founders of modern Wicca—particularly Gerald Gardner—whose pioneering work in this form of spirituality, drew inspiration for the Wiccan version of an altar from a variety of sources, many of which had been of popular interest during the English occult revival of the late 1800s and early 1900s.

One was the practice of "high magic," also referred to as "ceremonial magic."

This form of interaction with spiritual energies was used by groups like the Hermetic Order of the Golden Dawn, which was quite in vogue in esoteric circles just a few years before Gardner's time.

Another influence may have come from Masonic practices and similar secret organizations.

Gardner was also influenced by Aleister Crowley, a famous occult scholar and author of the day. All of these sources were in turn influenced by older medieval occult texts, many of which were themselves inspired by even older traditions and practices.

So although the altars of modern day Wiccans are relatively new incarnations, the spirit of the practice is indeed centuries old.

COMMON "TOOLS" AND THEIR ARRANGEMENTS

In Traditional Wicca—that is, the kind practiced by people who closely follow the "Gardnerian" tradition (or the "Alexandrian" tradition, named for Alex Sanders, another early pioneer), the altar is fairly elaborately laid out, with a designated place for everything on it.

The placements are based on correspondences related to the four cardinal directions (north, east, south, and west), but they also acknowledge left and right, as well as top and bottom.

The items themselves are symbolic and represent one or more of the forces in Nature that Wiccans recognize as contributing to the circumstances of our existence, including the four elements, the four directions, and the deities themselves (the Goddess and the God and/or aspects thereof).

Exact tools and arrangements vary from tradition to tradition, but almost all Wiccans will have the following items somewhere on their altar: statues or other representations of the Goddess and God; one or more candles; a chalice; a wand; an athame (ritual knife); a bowl of salt, sand or soil; a dish of water, and a bell.

Other possible items include a cauldron, a pentacle, and a variety of objects used for spellwork, such as crystals, cords, oils and herbs.

Covens performing group rituals will generally have a standard arrangement for their altar, which is based on the particular tradition that they follow, although "independent" covens might create their own traditional arrangement.

The same is true for solitary Wiccans, or even members of covens who have their own personal practice in addition to the coven gatherings.

Eclectic Wiccans are just that—eclectic. This means they can either follow an established altar arrangement or invent their own. They may or may not incorporate every single tool used by Traditionalists. Some are quite simplistic in their altar arrangements, preferring just three or four objects. This can be especially true for those who have smaller altars with limited space.

ALIGNING ENERGIES

As you've no doubt noticed by now, the objects found on the altar are referred to as "tools" in Wicca.

Some newcomers find this to be a rather odd word choice for a religious context. But the word "tools" underscores the Wiccan belief that we are working actively to co-create with the Goddess and the God for a spiritually rich and nature-oriented life.

Again, Wiccans are not just passive recipients of the benevolent energy of Nature—we also actively work to shape it. The tools of the altar are used to direct magical energies according to our will.

The way in which the tools are used—the order of the ritual actions and what each stands for—also varies from tradition to tradition and practitioner to practitioner.

However, the worship and magical work are not undertaken randomly. Each action and each object is deliberately representing some aspect of the relationship between the practitioner and the divine presence that the ritual calls into the space on the altar and in the sacred circle surrounding it.

This aspect of Wicca can be hard to grasp at first. The only way to really start to "get it" is to study and practice. For now, just know that millions of people wouldn't be doing these things in this way if it had no effect whatsoever on them or their lives.

Essentially, the point of the tools and all the ceremony is to focus personal energy and align it with the higher vibrations of universal energy.

The truth is that tools are not really strictly necessary—adept Wiccans can interact with this energy without them, simply by drawing on their personal power and focused attention. But as sensory creatures who learn from patterns, symmetry, symbols, etc., the use of tools is a great help in training and keep our focus where it needs to be—in the energetically charged space of the sacred circle.

And since the vast majority of Wiccans use these tools, we are joining up with the collective power of their energetic influence on the spiritual plane when we do so.

CREATING AN ALTAR OF YOUR OWN

So what does a Wiccan altar look like, exactly?

Like any other aspect of this diverse practice, the answer depends on the tradition being followed (or lack thereof), the preferences of the individual or coven, and, often enough, the available materials and available space.

Those groups and individuals lucky enough to be able to designate a permanent space for their altars are generally able to use very natural materials—stone is a popular option for outdoor altars, while wood works well both indoors and outdoors.

Some covens and solitaries prefer to keep it as simple and natural as possible—using the flattened surface of a dead tree trunk, for example. Others like to have a more ornate altar with elaborate carvings.

Indoor permanent altars can be made of just about anything, since weather isn't a consideration. Nonetheless, natural materials, like marble or wood, are still generally preferred over synthetic or processed materials like vinyl or formica.

Altars may be tall enough to work from standing up, or low enough to use from a sitting positions—in a chair or even on the floor.

Usually, the altar resides in the corner of the room until it's moved to the center for ritual and/or spellwork, though some Wiccans are fortunate enough to have a spare room with the altar permanently placed in the center.

Others may need to make do with just a portion of the room—which is no less effective, of course! The Goddess and God are not concerned with the size of your home or room, so don't ever feel inferior if your altar and tool collection are on the more humble side.

Many Wiccans don't actually have a permanent structure to use as an altar. Plenty of kitchen and coffee tables are temporarily "repurposed" for Sabbats, Esbats, and spellwork, which, again, is perfectly fine!

With a little imaginative thinking, however, you might be able to permanently repurpose a modest-sized trunk or chest of drawers, using the interior to store your magical tools, while not drawing unwanted attention to the altar from visitors or family members, if you're not open about your Wiccan practice.

Now is a good time to mention that any material object you wish to acquire for your spiritual purposes can be called to you through focused intention. Simply ask the powers that be (you can name the Goddess and/or the God, or whatever deity or other focal point makes sense to you) to aid you in finding what you need. Then, be sure to pay attention! Visit thrift stores, yard sales, and any other place where you know it's possible to discover what you're looking for.

In the meantime, you really don't have to wait until you have an altar to begin practicing Wicca. You can just use what you have at the moment, and start wherever it makes sense to you. You might even just sit on the floor, light a candle (being careful not to knock it over, of course!) and meditate on the concept of the Goddess and God, the power of nature, or whatever aspect of Wicca has drawn you to explore it further. There's no right or wrong way to begin, as long as you're following your heart!

THE ALTAR AND THE CIRCLE

Before we dive into setting up the altar and the variety of tools involved in enhancing your practice, it's essential to highlight the role of the circle.

Casting a circle is an important aspect of practicing Wicca and is done before ritual and spellwork.

You can imagine the circle being like a force field that keeps negativity and the mundane noise of everyday life from affecting the energy of your sacred space. It is a protective bubble that can be likened to the walls of a church, mosque, or synagogue—whatever is going on outside of the circle is sealed off.

Woven with your energy and the energy of the five elements of Earth, Air, Fire, Water, and Akasha (spirit), it is a powerful vortex where time can seemingly stand still when you are within it.

The circle is considered sacred ground from the very first revolution of casting until it is closed at the end of the ritual.

Each direction corresponds with a specific element: east for Air, south for Fire, west for Water, and north for Earth. Casting a circle is always done traveling deosil, or clockwise, typically beginning at due east. However, some Wiccans like to begin with the direction that their ruling element corresponds with, so if you're a water sign, for example, you would start with the west.

Traditionally, the Watchtowers (also known as the "Four Quarters")—one for each cardinal direction—are hailed for their power and protection. Each direction is invoked with a corresponding ritual tool that aligns with the direction's element.

If starting with the east, you'll walk the circle with incense to call on the Watchtower of the east with the element of air. Then for the south, you'll walk with a candle. For the west, you'll sprinkle water along the circle's borders—"drawing" the actual shape of the circle with the droplets. Finally, for the north, you'll draw the circle again by sprinkling salt along its borders.

Some Wiccans will make three passes of the circle for each cardinal direction and element, while others will limit it to one pass. It's also common to make a final pass to invoke Akasha, or "spirit," the fifth element. This all depends on your preferences and how strong your energy feels once your circle has been cast.

Think of it like winding a cord around you to protect you and your work—how "thick" does the cord need to be for you to feel completely comfortable?

When your ritual and/or spellwork is done, you will perform a rite to close the circle.

You begin with the same cardinal direction that you used to cast, but this time traveling widdershins (counterclockwise). Now, rather than invoking the Quarters, thank them for their participation and release them. Use your chosen ritual tool to disperse the energy by waving it away. It's recommended to use the same amount of passes as you did when casting.

The tools for casting a circle will depend upon how involved you want the process to be.

While many Wiccans follow the traditional manner by using a different 'tool' for each of the quarters and elements, others will find that using just one ritual tool, such as the wand or athame, will suffice. As with most aspects of ritual, this is up to you.

Below you will find a table that shows each direction's element and the best tool(s) for walking the circle after calling each quarter.

Cardinal Direction	Element	Casting Tool
East	Air	Incense, Resin on Charcoal
South	Fire	Candles, Torch (outside)
West	Water	Holy, Moon, Solar, Sea, or Tap Water
North	Earth	Sea Salt, Soil, Chalk, Pebbles
Center	Akasha (Spirit)	Ritual Tool (Wand/Athame) or Your Hands

In addition to these tools, you will also want something to mark the four directions of your circle.

Larger areas will accommodate pillar candles, and tiki torches work well outside. Lanterns are also excellent, but because you will want to work with actual fire when possible, try to consider the amount of space you can work with. Kerosene may be okay in the large living area of a home when you are the only one in the house, but if you are in your bedroom, you may want to invest in a few inexpensive battery-operated tealights, or real tealights in enclosed lanterns that cannot be bumped or light your robes on fire as you pass by.

Alternatively, if fire just isn't an option, you can use crystals or other stones to mark the quarters.

PLACING THE ALTAR

The altar is traditionally positioned to face the east point of the circle, but you can also place it in the cardinal direction that corresponds with your dominant element, or in the center of the circle.

As always, it's important to honor your personal intuition and preferences—the Goddess isn't so picky that she would reject your wanting to commune with her simply because you're facing the wrong way!

You will also want to take into account the purpose and form of your magical work when you set up your circle.

If you will be burning something in a cauldron or doing candle magic, perhaps the center of the circle would be safer than toward the edge, where embers could fly up into the curtains, bedding, or living room furniture. If you will be raising energy with chanting or circle dancing, better to put it off near the inner edge of your circle so you can move about without bumping your altar or tripping over it.

Remember, your altar will undoubtedly play host to at least one candle, a chalice with wine or juice, or a charcoal cake with powdered incense smoldering away, so you will need to keep safety and stability in mind when placing it within the circle.

SETTING UP YOUR ALTAR

The altar can have a wide variety of different layouts and tools. How your altar is set up will depend on practicality, space, the members (if any) who will be with you, and what type of Wicca you wish to practice.

If you really have no idea how to set up your altar, it can be useful to follow a traditional "blueprint." As with everything in Wicca, different practitioners have their own preferred methods, and so a wide variety of blueprints are available, including this standard layout below.

It's worth pointing out that a blueprint can help you find your bearings, but doesn't have to be followed perfectly. For example, if you're missing one of the "recommended" tools, use something else in its place, or leave a space. You can add and alter your altar layout as you gain experience. (An altar setup blueprint is included at the end of this section.)

The altar setup begins with representations of the deities at the top. These may be from a specific pantheon or simply represent a general Goddess and God.

The altar will also house cakes and/or ale, which are offerings that are taken in a way that reminds of the sacrament in the Catholic Church. Usually, these are enjoyed by the practitioner, so they should be kept on the opposite end from anything that is toxic or otherwise inedible, such as anointing oils or poisonous herbs.

Ritual tools that do not hold or touch these inedible items will sit either at the center of the altar or on the same side as the cakes and libations, depending on the space you have to work with.

Again, there are a wide variety of other tools that some practitioners will find essential, but if you're just getting started, the items in the above layout are enough to begin with.

Keep in mind that you don't have to have all of them in order to perform your first ritual. Wicca is very malleable, and you can adapt things to suit you in the manner you like. For example, if you have a wand, you don't necessarily need the athame, since either one can serve the functions of the other.

You can also switch out the arrangement of items for easier spellwork or divination. If something is going to be in your way using the layout above, improvise according to what works best for you.

Some people like to keep the center of the altar completely clear in order to focus more intently on spellwork, or perform divination with runes. Nothing here is set in stone. You just need to plug into the energy of the circle and work your rituals with focused good intention.

Altar Setup Blueprint

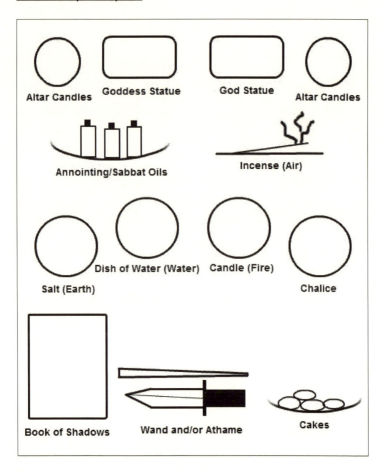

PART TWO

THE TOOLS OF WICCAN RITUAL AND MAGIC

THE BASICS

As you saw in the diagram in the previous section, there are many tools involved in a traditional Wiccan ritual.

Below you'll find a list of the most essential basics along with brief explanations of their use and, where appropriate, suggestions for acquiring them.

Don't feel pressured to rush out and purchase everything at once, however. Take your time and get to know your new tools gradually—they will serve you better in the long run if you do.

ALTAR CLOTH

Your altar might be a very special, ornately designed antique, or it might be something more mundane, like your living room coffee table.

Whatever the case, because of the materials you're working with—oils, herbs, incense, and candles—you will undoubtedly encounter some kind of mess at one point or another.

An altar cloth protects the surface of your altar from burns, wax, and oil staining. (For those whose altars are doing double-duty as an ordinary piece of furniture, it can also add some welcome energetic ambiance.)

It can be as plain or as pretty as you like, but you may want to stick to a fabric that's washable, and that you won't be heartbroken to have ruined by accident.

ALTAR CANDLES

Otherwise known as *illuminator candles*, altar candles are there for just this purpose: to illuminate your working surface.

You can use taper candles, but pillar candles are more stable and generally last much longer than tapers, not to mention the drip factor—although many tapers are advertised as being "drip-free," pillar candles are much more so.

For the altar, you will need at least two illuminator candles, which sit off to the sides at the top corners of the altar. These candles are traditionally white, which symbolizes purity and spirit.

DEITY REPRESENTATIONS

For many Wiccans, the deity representations are probably the most important part of the altar setup.

However, *which* deities you choose to represent, and *how* you represent them will depend on which form of Wicca you intend on practicing.

Those whose beliefs are rooted in the Gardnerian area of Wicca will likely follow the tradition of venerating a supreme Goddess and God, who embody all other deities, though some prefer to worship specific gods and goddesses from Egyptian, Celtic, Norse, or Greek pantheons.

Other traditions, particularly those within Dianic Wicca, place a great deal of emphasis on the power of the Goddess, and may use a single representation of the divine on their altars in the form of their patron goddess or the exalted Triple Goddess.

For those who work with specific goddesses and gods (generally viewed within Wicca as "aspects" of the supreme Goddess and God), the representations themselves are often visual images of the deity.

For instance, those who are followers of the Norse pantheon may worship Freyja and Odin with sculptures in their likeness. Others may feel connected to the Celtic gods and goddesses, opting to use engravings or paintings of The Morrigan and The Dagda for their altars.

This can be a nice touch, but if you don't have access to such specific images, you can opt to use two pillar candles as representation of the divine just as effectively. Find out which colors are most often associated with the deities you want to work with, and choose your candles accordingly.

As for those who don't work with specific deities, but rather wish to acknowledge the Goddess and God in general, it's traditional to use a silver candle for the Goddess and a gold one for the God.

But whether you're working with aspects or supreme deities, the representations should ideally be placed toward the center of the top of the altar.

The Goddess goes on the left, representing female, night, and all things hidden. The God, who signifies the day, masculinity, and the physical world goes on the right.

ATHAME

The athame is a short, ritual knife that resembles a simple dagger.

An influence from ceremonial magic, it is a representation of the element of air in the Golden Dawn tradition and fire in Gardnerian Wicca.

It typically has a black handle and a double-edged blade. Although it may have sharp edges, most practitioners keep a dull athame because it's not actually used as a cutting tool. (Note: some Wiccans opt for using a sword in place of a ritual knife, but this is best in large, usually outdoor spaces and with few people, in the interest of safety.)

When choosing an athame, be sure to spend some time holding each knife you're considering in your hand. Consider the carvings on the handle (if any), the colors, and whether it seems practical for your ritual space. Pick one that you can keep a firm grasp on while casting circles, drawing pentacles, or consecrating other tools. You don't want to have an unfortunate accident.

Take cost into consideration too. Some ritual knives are very extravagant, but you can turn any "ordinary" object into a ritual tool with the right energy and intent.

The most important thing to consider, of course, is how you feel with it in your hand—if the energy of the knife doesn't feel positive, then it's not likely meant for you.

WAND

Wands represent fire in some circles and air in others.

They're used for similar purposes as an athame, but can also be used specifically for working with spirits if you have both and want to differentiate.

Wands don't have to be large to hold tremendous power, either. In fact, anything that's more than 12 inches in length isn't going to be very practical.

Wands can be made of nearly any material, but in Wicca there is an emphasis on the earth being the origin of all tools. Metal, crystal, wood—these are the typical materials used for manufacturing wands.

There are gorgeous wands out there with crystal points fastened to their ends, as well as more rustic versions made of wood, with carvings and perhaps leather braiding. You may also come across wands that are simply a skinny length of a tumbled gem.

A great way to acquire the wand that's meant for you is by venturing out into the woods and moving through the trees until you come across a nice branch or twig that has already fallen to the ground. (You should always avoid ripping a living branch from the tree in order to respect nature and the Earth Mother.)

When you find one that speaks specifically to you, ask permission from the tree to take the branch for your work.

If you sense that permission has been granted (take note of how you feel physically in the moment if you're unsure), take the branch and leave an offering for the tree in thanks.

The branch is then yours to decorate as you please. There are some great DIY projects online for adding a crystal point to the wand, carving sigils into it, or wrapping it in tooled leather.

CHALICE

The chalice is a representation of the element of water and is used for offerings, or what we in Wicca call Cakes and Ale.

These offerings should be partaken of and given in thanks to the God and Goddess as you near the end of a ritual or spellwork.

The God and Goddess have lent their power to your work and prayers, provided you with the materials to make your charms and do spells, and are your constant guardians while you're in this life. Performing the Cakes and Ale ceremony is a traditional way to honor them for their support.

The chalice takes on the shape of a goblet or short-stemmed wine glass. It can be made of wood, metal, or glass. (Again, if it comes from the earth, it's a good choice.)

Often, you may see chalices that are plated in brass or silver. These look amazing when you first get them, but if you choose to use brass or silver, watch out for tarnish, as well as the acidity of whatever you drink from them, such as wine. Acid eats metal.

Of course, you don't *have* to drink beer or wine from your chalice. You can use fruit or vegetable juice, or just water, if you prefer.

Whatever liquid you choose, be sure to clean your chalice with a soft cloth and warm, soapy water before putting it away. If you decide to use silver cleaner or a polish, only use it on the outside, and be sure to rinse the surface clean. You don't want to inadvertently ingest chemicals.

CAKES AND PLATES

A cake plate can be any ordinary plate, or something special, like a piece of china.

It should always be kept separate from any other dishes, bowls, and tools that touch anything inedible—like poisonous herbs, oils, incense, or other ingredients for spellwork.

If you are on your own, you can use a small dish, but covens should get a large enough dish to hold an entire group's worth of cakes or other bite-size offerings.

As for the "cakes" themselves, they don't really have to be cakes.

Traditionally, witches would make oatcakes for this purpose, but you can make any sort of cookie or biscuit, or use fruit instead, or even chop up some veggies if that's more your style.

Covens may have their own preferences according their traditions (and any allergies), but solitary practitioners can go for whatever they feel comfortable with offering up.

The cakes sit on the same side of the altar as the chalice, ready for when the ritual is nearing its end.

It's often nice to simply enjoy your Cakes and Ale in quiet introspection. It can also be fun to sit and enjoy music and trance during the moments of thanks.

INCENSE
(AIR REPRESENTATION)

Incense is a grand representation of air that is usually carried around the circle when invoking the east and the element of air in circle-casting.

It's also used for consecration, purifying items, and in spellwork.

This item is placed near one of the illuminator candles, off to one side of the altar.

There are several different types of incense. Incense sticks are the most commonly available on the market. They can be bought nearly everywhere, but you will want to make sure that they contain all-natural ingredients as opposed to synthetic fragrances.

Never buy blends that contain only fragrance oils. Your incense should have a comprehensive ingredient list that contains items like essential oils, ground herbs, and resin.

You will also need an incense holder that you can easily stand your stick in. Look for one that catches ash for less mess, and less risk of burning holes in your altar cloth.

Incense cones are much like incense sticks. They're made of the same combustible material and burn slowly over a period of time. You will need a heat-proof dish that can catch ash for these as well, but they last a long time.

The same rules apply with cone incense when shopping around: all-natural ingredients are the only way to go.

Loose incense is generally the preferred type among Wiccans.

These blends of dried and crumpled herbs and wood shavings are mixed with oils or small granules of resin. They are quite fun to use, and very easy to make.

The only potential drawback is that you will need charcoal tablets to burn them on, as well as a very sturdy heat-proof dish or censer to place the charcoal in. (These accessories will be covered in the next section, below.)

Loose incense doesn't tend to burn for as long as other types, but it's got a very back-to-basics aesthetic since you can see literally every ingredient in the blend.

It's very important that loose, burning incense is not disturbed, since the smoldering bits of herbal oils and grounds can fairly easily ignite or burn holes in fabric and other surfaces.

Loose incense also comes in powdered form, which is less unpredictable when burning, but tends to burn even faster than the traditional loose variety.

Resins are another form of incense, which are not often found in shops that sell more conventional incense, but which have been used by Native Americans in their ceremonies for hundreds of years.

These sticky bricks are made with sap, dried herbs, woods, and oils and have very strong and clean fragrances. They also require charcoal and other accessories, described in the following section.

Finally, smudge sticks, while not technically considered incense, can be used for the same purpose.

They're made up of bundles of partially dried herbs that smolder well. The most common smudge sticks are made using sage, which is used in house cleansing and purification rites.

When casting a circle, it's best to leave the stick smoldering in a heatproof dish and use a feather to fan the smoke around. This will prevent embers from randomly dropping to the floor and burning things.

You can make your own smudge sticks too, using herbs that you think are most appropriate for your intended purpose for casting a circle or in devotion to a specific Sabbat.

You will need to make sure that they do not contain any noxious chemicals that would be harmful to inhale, so do your research before experimenting with smudge sticks.

Note: some people prefer not to use incense due to allergies and asthma that can flare up due to certain mixtures of oils and herbs, or even just the smoke in general. If this is the case, you can light a candle anointed with oil that represents air, and this will at least help to signify air in some manner without irritating your lungs.

CANDLE (FIRE REPRESENTATION)

You may have noticed from the example altar setup that in addition to the illuminator candles and the Goddess and God candles (if using), you will need another candle on your altar to represent fire.

This candle is traditionally carried around the circle during casting and used light the quarter candles that mark the four directions, as well as invoking the element of fire and the southern Watchtower.

You can use a color that's associated with fire—any shade of red or orange is lovely—and anoint it with an essential oil that corresponds with the fire element, if you like to go the extra mile in your rituals.

It would seem most practical to use a colored pillar or votive candle, but this, of course, depends on the size of your altar.

A taper, though it carries the risk of wax drippings, is slender enough to be a more comfortable fit on a smaller altar. Just make sure it's not so tall that it gets in your way.

DISH OF WATER (WATER REPRESENTATION)

A dish of water also sits atop the altar to represent the western element.

This can be water charged with the energy of the moon or sun, or another type of holy water, but pure water will do just fine.

When casting your circle, this is the water you will sprinkle as you make a pass and invoke the western Watchtower.

You don't need all that much—even just a quarter of a cup will do.

This water is not for drinking—it will be picking up a lot of different energies (and perhaps an accidental bit of herb, oil, or wax now and again) so it's best not to ingest it.

Your dish can be as plain or ornate as you like, but keep it with your other altar tools, rather than with your regular dishes.

DISH OF SEA SALT OR SOIL (EARTH REPRESENTATION)

Another small dish on the surface of your altar will contain your earth representation.

This can be soil, sea salt, or even small pebbles, which is a really nice touch for outdoor rituals.

You can sprinkle the sea salt or soil as you walk around the circle and invoke the earth element and the northern Watchtower. (Note: Whichever you use, you may want to sweep or vacuum it up once you've closed your circle, especially if you have pets.)

Like the water dish, this vessel should be kept for the one purpose only.

ANOINTING OILS

Anointing oils are essential oils—either single oils or blends—used in rituals for anointing the Goddess and God candles or statuettes, marking your third eye before divination, and more.

There is a wide variety of essential oils used in Wiccan ritual and spellwork, some of which have been used for spiritual purposes since the days of the Old Testament, where you'll find references to myrrh, cinnamon, cassia, and olive oils used for anointing sacred items.

You can find specially blended oils for use in magic at any Pagan shop, whether it be bricks-and-mortar or online.

Generally, the oil used for anointing deity candles and other altar tools is reserved for this purpose—oils used in other ritual work and/or spellwork are kept separately.

Because they are combustible, keep them away from heat sources, and always store oils in dark glass bottles.

When shopping for essential oils, always read the labels—never use anything with synthetic oils or "fragrance" oils.

YOUR BOOK OF SHADOWS

If you've just done your initiation rites, you may not have much of a Book of Shadows of your own yet.

However, it's a good idea to plan your rituals and enter them in a booklet as you are ready to perform them. If you want to do a spell, write it in your book, and refer to it during your work.

Your Book of Shadows is like a Wiccan journal that shows a record of your rituals and spells, information about Sabbats and Esbats, etc.—basically, any information you find to be important and/or helpful as you progress along your path.

Think of it like a script, which you will undoubtedly need until you get used to casting a circle, doing the Cakes and Ale, performing consecrations, and all of the other steps involved in ritual and spellwork.

Choose a notebook or journal that is portable, practical, and calls to you. It can be a good idea to use different books for different types of information if possible—for example, one for correspondences, one for Sabbat lore, etc., This can help keep you organized. Alternatively, you can also get multi-tabbed notebooks for the same purpose.

If you have each of the items described above, you can perform essentially every Sabbat and Esbat in an adequate manner.

Again, it might be nice to have everything you read about right off the bat, but it makes more sense to pace yourself. As you're learning and getting more comfortable with ritual protocol, it's fine to use what you have on hand—an old plate and cup that you can spare from the kitchen, for example.

Remember that the witches of old didn't have online pagan supply stores just a few clicks away—they got creative with what they had at their disposal, and you can, too.

FURTHER OPTIONS

Beyond the basics covered above, there are several other items that can enhance your ritual and spellwork—some add delightful energy, while others assist with practicality.

Some may be more "optional" than others, depending on whether you're joining a coven that has specific requirements, or working at your own discretion as a solitary Wiccan.

Remember that just as with the "basics," there's no law that states you have to go out and acquire everything at once. Take your time, explore, and see what feels right to you.

BROOM

You're likely already aware that, contrary to popular belief, the broom is not a method of transportation for witches.

In Wicca, as in many other cultures and religions, the broom is used to sweep out negative energy.

However, this isn't necessarily a physical sweeping. It's merely a way of preparing a place for sacred spiritual exercises and rituals.

The broom can also be used to help close the circle once you're ready to dismiss the quarters—it can be highly effective at dissipating the energies of the work.

During ritual, the broom will usually sit to the side of the altar.

You can get a hand-made "novelty" broom or use an actual functioning one, but whatever you choose, it should only be used in ritual, so don't just grab one from your hall closet—with the possible exception of a decorative broom, this is one tool that shouldn't be "repurposed" for magic.

As associated with all things witchy as the broom may be, this can be considered an optional tool, depending on your preferences. If you feel that your circle-casting and circle-closing methods are adequate without a need for this particular step, so be it.

But it can be both a fun and calming way to clear energy from a room.

A WITCH'S BELL/ DEVIL DRIVER

The witch's bell, or devil driver, is used for several purposes.

Firstly, as its namesake implies, drives away negative energy and malevolent spirits before working in your circle or performing certain rites.

It is also used to call to the God and Goddess.

Some Wiccans will ring the bell three times before beginning work at their altar and after casting the circle. Others will ring the bell thrice before casting their circle to declare the whole ritual to have started.

The bell can also be used in prayer to bring attention to your calls, and it is also used to seal a spell (like the words 'so mote it be').

Witch's bells are made like the bells the town crier in most old cities would use.

They are nearly always made of heavy-gauge metal and a solid handle. They can be brass or steel and may be decorated with silver or gold plating, and etchings and/or engravings.

They are available in different colors, and should have a gorgeous ringing sound.

You can usually tell the quality of the bell by the weight, so be sure to look for this spec if purchasing yours online.

A PENTACLE SLAB

Many Wiccans will have a round pentacle slab on their altars.

These can be made of wood, metal, or stone, and they often have intricate carvings.

They are used to bring added protection to rituals and the circle in general, and to charge ingredients for spellwork. (However, you can draw pentacles in the air above your spells, tools, and the like, in place of passing them over the pentacle, and there are many, many ways to charge spell ingredients.)

You can make your own pentacle slab, or purchase one from a Pagan store.

Just be sure, if you purchase an ornately carved one with sigils in addition to the pentacle symbol, that you know what the sigils stand for. You don't want to be invoking any unwanted energies into your spells or rituals without knowing it.

INCENSE ACCESSORIES

No matter what type of incense you use, you'll need something heat-proof to hold it in and to catch the ash, so technically this item isn't "optional."

But the simpler incense types—sticks and cones—are definitely less fuss than the more traditional and elaborate forms, so if you're not inclined to spend much time, money, or energy on incense, these are probably your best bet.

Stick incense works best in a "boat," or long tray with a hole in one end for inserting the non-burning end of the stick. The ash should land on the tray as the stick burns down.

Cone incense can be burned in any type of shallow, heat-proof dish—even a small plate will do, if you don't mind possible scorch marks. The best holders for cone incense have three legs, which is a homage to the three states of being: mind, body, and spirit.

Although you can go for a brass or copper holder, keep in mind that it will heat up, which is risky when you're walking the circle with it or otherwise moving it about. For this reason, some people prefer an ashtray, abalone shell, or a stone dish.

For burning resins, loose incense, and powdered incense, you'll need a couple of additional ingredients.

The first is charcoal cakes or tablets. There are definite safety precautions to take when using charcoal—most obviously, avoiding the danger of fire and of using the wrong type of charcoal.

Charcoal briquettes are not the same thing as the tablets used to burn incense and herbs. Those are for outdoor barbecuing and they let off some extremely toxic fumes and byproducts when they're burnt, so you could poison yourself really badly by making a mistake with them.

Furthermore, make sure that your charcoal cakes or tablets do not contain saltpeter. If they do, they will release harmful inhalants as they burn. The trick to find out if yours have saltpeter is by watching to see if there are sparks when you light one. If so, throw them away, and go for another variety with ingredients clearly listed on the packaging.

Sand is another necessity if you are working with loose or powdered incense and resins.

It's excellent for absorbing heat, extinguishing flame and embers, and providing a safe bed for smoldering charcoal cakes to sit on. You can gather sand for free from beaches, riverbeds, or even a playground. If you don't live near places like these, try visiting your local gardening store—they may give you a good deal on a couple of pounds.

To put it altogether, you lay the charcoal on top of a generous layer of sand in a heat and shatterproof dish and sit the dish on a trivet to keep it from heating up the altar surface too much. (Some people like to use small cauldrons for this purpose.) Then you ignite the charcoal and place the incense on top.

Another, optional ingredient to add to the process is mica.

Mica is a type of rock that makes for a perfect "stove top" for burning oils, loose incense, powders, and resins, if you find that sitting them on the charcoal burns them away too fast. Your mica tablet should easily sit on top of the charcoal and act as a barrier for the intense heat. It will essentially simmer your herb mixture instead of scorching it.

CAULDRON

Heat and shatterproof dishes are very useful for incense, candles, and more, but a cauldron is an invaluable part of your altar tool setup if you can get your hands on one.

They're wonderful for fire spells and potions, and can do double-duty as incense holders, as mentioned above.

Cauldrons come in all sorts of sizes and designs, but the double-handled classic design works well. Its curved edges help contain candle flames, and because most are still made of cast iron, you don't have to worry about it shattering.

Your cauldron should have feet, and if it's small enough to sit on the altar, it should sit on a trivet to keep it from damaging your altar-top.

CANDLE SNUFFER

Another invaluable tool to have at your disposal is a candle snuffer.

While it is optional, consider that there are beliefs in several cultures around the world that blowing out a candle with your breath is disrespectful.

Some people use their fingers to snuff out candles, and others clap their hands over them, hoping that the downward draft will be enough to extinguish the flames. These can be hazardous due to the risk of burns and knocking things over or lighting sleeves on fire.

If you aren't that much of a superstition follower, you might not mind blowing out your candles, but you risk blowing melted wax off of them as well, which can stain walls, ruin fabric, and splatter quite astoundingly in every direction.

It's best to be gentle and cautious with candles in every respect. A candle snuffer can make this easy.

LONG MATCHES OR BARBECUE LIGHTER

Because lighting candles, incense, and charcoal can be really difficult if you can't reach or need sustained flame, it's best to invest in some long-handled matches or a barbecue lighter.

This allows you to hold the flame for longer periods of time against cone incense or charcoal—which can take awhile to ignite.

You can also reach into those deep candle jars that you might be using for quarter candles, and access the candles on your altar much more easily.

The best part? No more burned thumbs or soot on the cuffs of your clothes!

WRITING UTENSIL (PEN OR PENCIL)

It never hurts to have a pen on hand when doing rituals or spells within the circle.

If you haven't written the work out in advance in your Book of Shadows, you will probably want to record what you're doing, so keep a pen hooked onto it.

BASKETS

Baskets are definitely not a necessity when working at your altar, but they're perfect for carrying extra items for Sabbat rituals and spellwork without cluttering up your altar or requiring disorganized armloads of items.

It's fairly easy to find inexpensive baskets at craft stores. They make for excellent and elegant storage containers for your altar tools, too!

BUCKET OF WATER

The inclusion of a container of water is more for safety than any other purpose.

You will have at least a few candles going during rituals, so you'll want to have an emergency water source—or alternatively, a small fire extinguisher, should something go wrong. You never know when you'll unknowingly drop a spark of incense, inadvertently light your robes on fire, or ignite curtains when a breeze whips up.

NEXT STEPS

Now that we've covered both the essential and the optional tools for use in ritual and spellwork, it's time to give some thought to how you might enhance your practice by enhancing your appearance.

As always, take the information below as suggestions, rather than rules, and adopt into your practice what feels appropriate for you.

RITUAL WEAR

Many religions involve some type of ritual clothing that officiants wear when performing rites of any kind.

Think about monks and priests—or nuns, many of whom wear their special garments every day. You can also look to the "church clothes" that most mainstream Christians wear each Sunday to see that ritual garments are held to be important.

While special clothing and/or jewelry are not at all necessary for participation in Wicca—at least not for solitaries—it can boost your confidence in your own energy to don something specifically designated for spiritual occasions.

When used appropriately, ritual wear can enhance the energy of your ritual space, add power to your work, and protect you from negativity.

Here are a few of the things that Wiccans might wear when in the circle.

PENTACLE

Yes, some practitioners will already have a pentacle on their altar, but most Wiccans will have a pentacle hanging around their neck during rituals as well. In fact, most Wiccans wear the pentacle quite regularly.

It is a symbol of protection, elemental magic, the soul, and completeness. The five points of the star each represent the five elements (Earth, Air, Fire, Water, and Akasha, aka spirit).

The pentacle doesn't belong to Wicca alone, of course. Other religions acknowledge the spiritual significance of this symbol, which has been featured in poetry, stone work, stained glass, and on the spires of many places of worship in the older age.

Unfortunately, a related symbol—the inverse pentagram—has been adopted by contemporary Satanists and is therefore considered to be an image of evil. Wiccans do not believe in the Christian construct of "the Devil" and this purported figure has no place in Wiccan spirituality.

Nevertheless, because the word "pentagram" has such a negative association, Wiccans use the term "pentacle," which emphasizes the circle drawn around the five-pointed star.

In any event, as mainstream as the pentacle has become within some circles, not all Wiccans wear one publicly. Many still keep it hidden when they are to avoid stares, confrontations, and observe the tradition of keeping their practice of magic a mystery.

Some covens only permit members to wear a plain pentacle, and not until they have been initiated.

If you're solitary, you may also wish to begin with a small, plain pentacle as you begin your practice, moving to a more ornate version once you feel comfortable with your progress, as a way of honoring your personal spiritual journey.

There are very beautiful pentacles out there made with gold, precious and semi-precious gems, and engravings, but there are also really pretty pewter kinds out there too.

You will want to make sure that the pentacle you get doesn't contain any nickel or metals that can cause irritation to your skin, and if you're secret about your faith but wish to wear one anyway, try to consider its size as well as the quality of the chain or cord for easy concealment.

GEMSTONE JEWELRY

Although purely optional, jewelry featuring crystals and other mineral stones is great for amplifying your spells and rituals.

Many practitioners have specially designated crystal jewelry for ritual work. Others choose stones that coincide with the work they are about to do within the circle on a given night. (This is why learning your stone correspondences is an important aspect of your journey into the world of Wicca.)

You can find all sorts of crystal jewelry in brick-and-mortar stores and online—they don't even need to be Pagan or "New Age" establishments.

Do make sure you're dealing with a reputable business though, as certain stones are sometimes found to be imitations—for example, "fake citrine" is produced when amethyst is heated to a certain temperature.

You don't need to wear everything in your jewelry box for a single ritual (though you certainly can if you like!). A simple bracelet of Tiger's Eye beads, a ring set with Jade, or a Lapis Lazuli pendant on a chain will do just fine.

Some crystal stores sell cords with tiny wire "baskets" attached, into which you can simply place the crystal of your choice.

Just be sure to wear pieces that have meaning for you and, ideally, correspond to the aims of your ritual and/or spellwork.

JEWELRY WITH SIGILS

Jewelry with sigils is often made from precious metals and may or may not feature gemstones.

Many sigils are for planets, elements, zodiac symbols, or other significant representations that are important to one's work.

If you decide to wear anything with a sigil other than a pentacle, be sure that you know exactly what it stands for and what its use is in Wicca. You don't want to wear something that has malicious meaning attached to it or muddle the meaning of a spell with mismatched energies.

As with other metal jewelry, you will want to keep your eye out for knock-offs and items made with nickel or other irritating materials.

RITUAL ROBES

Ritual robes can be a wonderful choice for those who wish to come to their Goddess and God in a very reverent manner.

We all know that you could be wearing burlap and approach your creator without causing offense, but it adds power to your magic and ritual work when you feel the part that much more.

Ritual robes can be custom-made or purchased in off-the-rack sizes and should not be confused with cloaks, which function as a covering rather than a main garment.

Robes come in many colors and materials, but you should be weary of long and flowing sleeves and flammable fabrics. You wouldn't want to light yourself on fire while spiral dancing or walking the circle, so be thinking about your particular ritual space, in addition to fit and comfort, when choosing your robes.

Again, unless you are a part of a coven with specific requirements, the choice is yours whether to use them or not.

CLOAKS

Cloaks are well-suited to outdoor rituals for Sabbats and for when doing magic outside on a cold night. They come in several styles and may or may not have sleeves or hoods.

Like ritual robes, cloaks can be custom-made or purchased off-the-rack.

If you're particularly keen to have a powerful, one-of-a-kind cloak, you might find a Pagan seamstress who will take your measurements and work magic into its creation.

Wherever you get your cloak, be practical about fabric and color—white robes and cloaks will often end up getting stained by oils, soiled by dirt, ash, or a number of other things while outdoors, and they don't always wash completely clean.

Furthermore, cloaks are often dry-clean-only due to the materials used to make them, so make sure this is doable for you.

Again, you don't *have* to wear anything special when in the circle (unless you belong to a coven, in which case you'll need to respect their traditions, of course.)

Some Wiccans wear nothing when performing rituals behind closed doors or in total seclusion, and others wear what they please.

Keep safety in mind, and follow your intuition when it comes to deciding on ritual wear.

As long as what you choose is comfortable, appropriate, and suits you, you have nothing to fret over.

TOOLS AND INGREDIENTS FOR SPELLWORK

In addition to the tools used in formal ritual described above, there is a wide range of very useful items for those Wiccans wishing to practice magic.

Some are fairly obvious—candles, for instance—while others may not have crossed your mind if you're new to Wicca and/or spell-casting, such as ribbons or squares of fabric.

Magic can take many different forms in Wicca, but the main branches of this ancient art revolve around candles, crystals, herbs, "spellcrafts"—the making of charms and other magical items—and divination. Below is a list of staple tools and ingredients to get you started in these and other forms of magic.

If yet another list of things to acquire in order to practice Wicca feels overwhelming at this point, just remember that these are optional, and that you should follow your intuition regarding where—or even whether—to start.

Not all Wiccans actually practice magic. Some were simply drawn to honor nature in the special way that the religion of Wicca offers, and choose to leave it at that.

If you do wish to pursue spellwork in your personal practice, don't be afraid to start small.

Perhaps you want to work with candle spells for awhile before moving onto crystals. Or perhaps you don't feel drawn to crystals at all, in which case, there's no need to acquire any!

The items described below have been helpful to many, many Wiccans on their journey toward becoming adept at magical practice.

Take a look, listen to your gut, and start with what makes sense to you. You can always return to this resource to try new things as you grow in your practice.

PARCHMENT

When we speak of parchment in Wicca, we aren't referring to the kind you would use to line a cake pan.

Parchment is paper that can be written on and burned or buried.

You can find parchment that's specially-made and pressed with flowers in it, which is good for those who like to use flower correspondences in their spells.

BOLINE

A boline is a special knife that's used for spells and other practical purposes. It is separate and very different from an athame, which is meant just for rituals.

The boline is a single-bladed knife that usually has a white handle.

Some bolines are very ornate (much like athames), but this almost always depends on the type of Wicca you practice and whether you are on your own or in a coven.

You use the boline for cutting, carving, and slicing ingredients in preparation for spells and rituals.

CANDLES

You can never have too many candles when practicing Wicca, particularly when it comes to spellwork.

The best places to find good deals on taper candles are discount stores, where you can often find a dozen of one color for a few dollars at the most. You could easily come home with several different colors of candle for spells and rituals for under twenty dollars.

You can also buy special 7-day candles that have notches for sections of one day worth of burning (but you can carve the notches yourself using your boline, too).

Specially charged candles are more expensive, but they carry greater power. It may be worth looking into these, particularly for beginners who are just trying out candle magic for the first time.

CRYSTALS AND OTHER MINERAL STONES

Crystals and stones are powerful items for magic for those who resonate with these Earth energies.

They all have different correspondences to planets, elements, and herbs.

Each stone also has specific purposes that it helps with, so before you purchase stones, it can be useful to do some research—there are many books and online resources detailing crystals and their magical properties.

As mentioned earlier, beware of counterfeit crystals—rarer ones like amber and jet are sometimes just dyed glass.

INCENSE, DRIED HERBS, AND ESSENTIAL OILS

You might have already caught on to the fact that different herbs have different magical properties, and just like crystals, they also have different planetary and elemental associations.

This means you can use various combinations of incense, dried herbs, and essential oils for various spells.

You can also grow your own herbs to make tinctures, infusions, dried herb bundles, and other products with your harvest, which saves money and adds extra magical power to your creations.

MAGIC CORD AND RIBBON

Magic cord and ribbon can be used for different purposes based on their colors.

Typically, you would use cordage and ribbons in binding spells, Beltane celebrations, and for tying up sprigs of herbs for asperging, drying your own fresh herbs, and knot magic.

DIVINATION TOOLS

Runes, tarot cards, scrying tools, tea leaves—these are all means of divination. Most of the time, practitioners will attempt to learn and master one method before moving onto another.

You may also find that your first divination method doesn't feel right for you, so try to start off simply. Purchase an inexpensive set of runes, or a smaller and easier scrying tool like a mirror or reflecting dish, instead of a crystal ball.

Tarot decks are another popular option. For beginners, try using a basic deck like the Rider-Waite deck to learn from.

A HAND DRUM OR RHYTHMIC MUSIC

Music is an extremely powerful vehicle for spirituality, and when doing chants, spiral dancing, raising energy, or celebrating Sabbats, nothing puts you in the correct frame of mind better than rhythmic music or your own instrument for playing.

A hand drum is great for chants and celebrations, especially because you don't have to be Mozart to use and enjoy it.

Meditation CDs are also great for listening to when you have trouble grounding and centering before casting your circle.

Whatever you choose to play or listen to, be sure that it's peaceful, gentle, and free of negativity.

MORTAR AND PESTLE

The mortar and pestle is an invaluable tool, both in the kitchen and in the circle.

They grind up herbs and fuse ingredients together so well, and their heavy stone construction makes them very sturdy.

It is best to get one that is wider in diameter to allow for larger mixes and spells.

Note: you will need to keep a separate mortar and pestle set for use in the circle—one that is never used in the kitchen—in order to prevent cross-contamination with any toxic or otherwise poisonous substances used in magic. Better to be safe than sickened!

EMPTY BOTTLES AND JARS

Jars and bottles are important due to their versatility and usefulness in spells and rituals, and for making potions, glamories, and more.

Often, you can simply repurpose your emptied food jars that would otherwise land in the recycling bin, but for some purposes, you may need to purchase a particular size, shape, or color.

It's best to have small vials for potions; small bottles with darker glass for oil blends and homemade perfumes; and large jars for large spells, storing dried herbs and incense, and making items like holy water, moon water, and solar water.

As with the mortar and pestle, you will want to have separate jars for separate purposes. Inedible herbs and poisonous oils should never come in contact with any vessels you wish to eat or drink from.

To ensure that no cross-contamination occurs, get labels for all jars and bottles used in magic.

MULTI-TAB NOTEBOOKS

Multi-tab notebooks are great for rough copies of spells, rituals, and working documents you would like to later organize and enter into your Book(s) of Shadows.

Multi-tab notebooks are best because you can keep Sabbat rituals, poetry, recipes, and spells separated for easier sorting.

You can also turn these into a Book of Shadows by transferring the information to a more permanent book, but this is up to you.

DIFFERENT COLORS OF JOURNALS

A Book of Shadows is a definite necessity for Wicca practitioners, but if you want to stay as organized as possible, you can keep different books for different areas of practice or study.

Simply do as described above: keep rough copies of your work, and periodically enter it with all of the tweaks and notes that you add as you learn and grow into each corresponding book.

Perhaps green could be herbalism. White could be for Sabbat rituals.

FABRICS AND SEWING MATERIALS

If you will be working with poppets, talismans, herb sachets, or dream pillows, you will need to invest in a few pieces of fabric and some basic sewing materials.

You don't have to have a sewing machine or be an adept tailor. Basic items like needles, thread, embroidery floss, scissors, and pins will do.

PART THREE

FINDING, PURCHASING, AND PREPARING YOUR TOOLS

BUYING AND PURCHASING WICCA TOOLS

In this section, I want to take a closer look at buying and purchasing your Wiccan supplies.

The witches of centuries ago wouldn't have had the luxury of superstores for buying their supplies—and certainly not the internet! They would have sourced their materials from nature.

While many Wiccans prefer to do this, it's undoubtedly much easier to drop by your local store to buy everything you need—usually at reasonable cost, too.

How you find your supplies is completely your decision, but don't feel the need to break the bank. Extravagant items aren't always better, and it pays to spend time finding items and supplies that resonate with your energies rather than throwing money at the problem.

PURCHASING SUPPLIES IN PERSON

Although your quest for Wiccan tools will most likely begin on an Internet search engine, you will quickly find that there are plenty of places within your community to obtain items for your work and studies.

Libraries can be great resources for books (which are expensive to buy outright) on many subjects of interest to Wiccans.

Gem shops will have crystals and tumbled or raw stones. They might also have pendulums, crystal balls, and other treasures.

And candles can be found in all kinds of places, from gift shops to big-box stores.

You may not find a new age one-stop-shop for all of your needs, but you can source many places right where you live. All you need is an open mind and a way to get around.

Wherever you go, take advantage of being physically present in the store to "feel out" the items you're considering buying.

While this is generally easier to do in a new age or gift shop than a big-box store (where there's much more "sensory overload" to compete with your intuition), you can always take moment to be still within yourself while holding the item.

If you feel any negativity, put it back down and keep searching. You'll know in your gut when you've found the right tool just for you.

PURCHASING SUPPLIES ONLINE

Purchasing supplies online for your spells and rituals can be somewhat risky.

You can do all of the research in the world, but you may not expect to be swindled by unscrupulous sellers on some sites, and false advertising happens everywhere.

The popular "scorpion in amber" talisman is a great example of this.

Someone with less common sense might wonder how so many scorpions happened to all get trapped in so much petrified tree resin at once. Obviously, the vast majority of these products are made of orange glass. (The scorpions probably aren't real either.)

The same thing happens with jet, and angle-cut plexiglass can look just like quartz crystal when it's shown in an online photo

The best way to fend off being taken advantage of when purchasing tools online is by reading reviews. Beware of a site with too many glowing 5-star reviews, however, since these are usually farmed out to people looking to make a few bucks online in exchange for falsified buyer feedback.

Look for reviews that mention pros and cons of the items or the overall quality of the business. You will also want to stick to reputable and secure sites that have been around for a while.

Pay attention to the weights and dimensions of what you're ordering, as well.

It's funny and sad when you open up a package and find that the gorgeous wand with the crystal point you ordered is only 4 inches long.

Don't be afraid to shop around either. The Internet has a truckload of options for purchasing magic items and ritual tools, and you can get amazing deals from quality sources if you look for them.

Finally, and as always, listen to your intuition.

If, while looking at pentacles on a particular website, you get a sinking feeling or any other kind of less-than-positive sense about the prospect of buying, just say no!

Thank your sixth sense for guiding you, and move on.

CONSIDER THE ITEM'S ORIGINS

In today's global marketplace, just about anything can be manufactured and shipped from incredible distances.

And although in the Western world we've largely eradicated the "sweatshop" conditions of earlier times, it's no secret that workers in other countries are not treated fairly or even humanely in many cases.

Furthermore, many companies in developing parts of the world are decades behind in terms of following environmentally sound practices. (Most first-world companies have very far to go on that score as well.) Supporting companies that treat their workers, and/or the environment, in negative ways is something that all ethical shoppers ideally try to avoid.

Wicca's spiritual and ethical framework adds extra weight to this matter.

Acquiring objects that were sourced and/or manufactured in a harmful manner is not very conducive to the energy we strive to commune with in ritual and spellwork. (Of course, regardless of where your tools come from, you will still have to remember to clear and consecrate them in order to get rid of the energy of all who have been involved in the creation, shipping, and sale of each item. We'll discuss this in detail below.)

Unfortunately, it can be nearly impossible to know everything you'd want to know about the origins of your purchases.

You can't know everything that happens in the mines where your gemstones are pulled from the rocks, and there isn't always a lot of information about a given company's labor conditions.

However, you can do your part by researching as much as you can.

Run an internet search on specific manufacturers to look for any negative press regarding environmental or labor practices. Look for businesses and products with Fair Trade certification—this label almost always ensures that both workers and the environment are being treated well.

Finally, support local businesses as much as you can. Environmentally sound consumerism starts with thinking locally vs. globally.

When you purchase something from a local, independent, non-chain business, you support your community and your environment, rather than the multinational global conglomerates who really don't need your business in order to thrive.

So consider beginning your search for tools as close to home as possible, and don't be afraid to ask your local retailers about the ethical origins of the products they sell!

AFFORDABLE OR EXTRAVAGANT?

It may be tempting, as an enthusiastic new Wiccan, to go on a shopping spree and buy the finest and fanciest tools you can find.

Indeed, there are many new age stores and online retailers with beautiful, ornate, and *very* expensive wands, cauldrons, athames, and the like.

However, there's no need to put a strain on your finances while seeking to grow in your spirituality.

Your tools don't have to be "top-of-the-line." They don't even have to be store-bought. The important thing is that they work well for you.

Nonetheless, there is something to be said for quality. Certain items deserve a higher price than others.

Consider patchouli oil, which is generally more expensive than lavender or lemon oil, because it takes a larger amount of the actual plant to produce essential oil.

If you pay too little for patchouli, you may think you're getting a great deal only to find out when it arrives that it's just fragrance oil.

Likewise, the price of metals like steel, copper, and gold have gone up tremendously in recent years, so tools made of these materials are going to run more than pewter, aluminum, or gold and silver-plated tools would.

Be aware that cheaper magical items can be made of poor materials or with techniques that cut corners, so you may run the risk of buying a second of the same thing at a higher price from somewhere else sooner than is worth it.

Simple items like cordage, ribbon, sewing supplies, candles, and more can be bought for cheap without being a problem, but don't try to scrimp on your bell or boline if you feel that they might not last.

Again, reviews are your friend when looking at tools like these. That way you can gauge whether the price and the quality seem to match.

WAYS TO SAVE MONEY FOR RITUALS AND SPELLWORK

There are several ways to save money in your pursuit of Wiccan tools and supplies. Some require more effort than others, but there is always extra magical value in hard work done with good intention.

Below are a few ways that Wiccan practitioners save money on items for their spells and Sabbats.

Gardening is perhaps the best way to save money on magical items. Wiccans know that you can get so much more out of gardening than just a few herbs for cooking.

With a little soil, a couple of flower pots, seeds, and some elbow grease, you can have a supply of magical herbs and flowers for a variety of purposes.

If you dry your herbs, you can make your own dream pillows, incense, smudge sticks, potpourri, tinctures, toiletries, and teas. Partially dried herbs can be used for asperging (using herb bundles to sprinkle water over an object or area), and if you know anything about steam distillation and have the equipment, you can make your own essential oils and use the hydrosol (leftover liquid) for things like rose water. Fresh herbs can be used in spells, too!

If you like crystals and other mineral stones and imagine that you would frequently use them in your magic, study your surrounding area's geology. You may be surprised at how many excellent sources for raw gemstones are right in your backyard.

Rockhounding is one way to collect gems in your vicinity. Typically, there will be a list of known dig sites and the specific minerals and crystals that have been pulled from them. You can also find agates and other treasures while combing beaches and the banks of rivers.

Hiking may provide you with an opportunity to pick up pieces of driftwood that could be carved into a guardian statue to place in front of your home, or a fallen tree branch might serve as a staff or a wand.

You can also do your own DIY projects with cloth if you like to sew. Altar cloths, ritual robes, sachets, talismans, dream pillows, and poppets all cost more to purchase ready-made.

You can even make your own magical soaps, shampoos, lotions, and candles for a fraction of the cost, if you consider how long a brick of beeswax or castile soap can last.

Those who just aren't "DIY-inclined" can still find good deals on many tools and magical items by looking for online sales and especially through stores' clearance categories.

Most new age shops will have sales right before Sabbats, with useful items at major discounts, and having an online ordering account can mean further member discounts.

You should also take a look at the different shipping deals stores have. Some will have lower purchase thresholds than others, and that can mean a lot of cash off of what you would normally pay if you have a heavy order.

Used bookstores and flea markets are two more resources for new Wiccans. There are always people who take their older and unwanted books in for trade or store credit, and some who decide that Wicca isn't for them after all will bring boatloads of books in for you to benefit from later. Indeed, the new age sections in most bookstores are loaded with amazing finds at great prices.

In regards to flea markets, some of the vendors will specialize in things like aromatherapy or incense-making. Because you can generally buy in bulk quantities, you'll save a lot of money over ordering from an online store.

Let's not forget that networking can be another useful tool in acquiring items at good prices.

You may be quite the seamstress, and a new Wiccan friend might have a passion for making gemstone jewelry. Swaps, trades, and friendly discounts are always out there. To find ways to meet other Wiccans in your area, you can look to the Internet where meet-ups and community groups are listed.

Finally, always remember that the Goddess and God aren't really interested in how much you paid for your chalice or ritual robes.

Listen to your inner voice, and you may find that the most expensive tools aren't as impressive as you first believe.

If you're having a hard time acquiring something that you feel would be beneficial for your practice, you can always work a spell to bring it into your life. It's really up to you!

CLEARING AND CONSECRATING YOUR TOOLS FOR RITUAL AND SPELLWORK

Once you've found your perfect wand, pentacle, athame, etc., it's important to perform a ritual to clear it of its former energy, and consecrate it in the name of the divine.

This is a vital part of practicing Wicca, because Wiccans know that everything on Earth is made of energy, and interactions between people and (seemingly) inanimate objects leave energetic imprints on both.

If you've ever walked into an old building and felt a distinctly different mood take over the atmosphere, you've experienced an energetic imprint. In fact, often enough when we say a house is "haunted," we're really just picking up on residual energy from past occupants and past events, rather than actual entities hanging around waiting to "spook" us.

Along these same lines, lingering energies from people who handled your tool before you acquired it can affect the quality of your ritual worship and spellwork. In fact, for those who are particularly sensitive to energy, just about any new acquisition can wreak a bit of energetic havoc.

A new dining table, for example, may look great in your home, yet you find yourself feeling restless when you try to sit down to eat. It may be that the person who delivered the table was dealing with a personal crisis and therefore very anxious when handling it. Or perhaps the wood was harvested in a manner destructive to the forest.

Whatever the reason, if you're feeling unsettled, heavy, melancholy, or any other unpleasant emotion or sensation around a particular object, this is a good indicator that you need to clear it of its residual energy.

When it comes to tools used in rituals and spellwork, it's essential that you perform this step in order to achieve the energetic and material results you're seeking.

For example, consider how it would be if a family member who's been down in the dumps came to you to do a happiness spell. You wouldn't want to use candles with the tired and toiling energy of a disgruntled worker who was having a very bad day when she placed them on the shelf at the store. You'd be bringing someone else's baggage to your family member's work, which would almost certainly cancel out any positive energy you're trying to manifest!

Indeed, a few moments of your time can make all the difference in your work if you've cleared and consecrated each of your tools.

A CLEARING AND CONSECRATION RITUAL

It's important to recognize that clearing and consecrating, while generally done in the same sitting, are two different steps.

Clearing removes residual energy, as discussed above.

Consecrating actually programs the innate energy of the object to for the purposes you intend. In Wicca, this means joining the energy of the object with the forces of the divine, usually as represented by the Goddess and the God.

For this ritual, you will follow the altar setup provided earlier in this guide. You may want to use soil or sand rather than sea salt if cleansing crystals or other mineral stones, depending on the stone's hardness. (Salt can pock the surface of softer stones.)

Be sure that you have gathered up all of the items you wish to consecrate.

__Note:__ if you're just starting out, you clearly run into a bit of a chicken-and-egg dilemma with this ritual. How can you use your dish of water to clear and consecrate your athame when you haven't yet cleared and consecrated your dish of water? Don't worry about following the instructions below to the letter when this is the case—you have to start somewhere!

Choose the tool you feel is most important to clear and consecrate first, and go from there, improvising until you've gotten to all of them. For example, if you haven't cleared and consecrated your wand, use your hand for those parts in the ritual. Trust that your own personal energy will do the trick, and that the Goddess and God are working with you, welcoming you into the Wiccan way.

Steps:

Begin by casting your circle. When you are ready to begin, take up the first item, and hold it up over your altar, while saying:

> *"I hereby cleanse this (item) in the name of the God and Goddess.*
> *May all negative and unwanted energies depart from it here and now!"*

Place the item in the center of your altar, and draw a pentacle over it with your wand, athame, or your hand, while saying:

> *"In the name of the element of spirit,*
> *I dedicate you to the divine.*
> *May you be used to harm none*
> *and respect the law of three."*

Next, take up your burning incense or smudge stick, and pass the item through its smoke.

> *"In the name of the element of air,*
> *I dedicate you to the divine.*
> *May you be used with and for insight,*
> *bringing joy and clear knowledge."*

After this, you will move to your fire candle on your altar. Quickly pass the item over the flame (or through it, if it's highly flame-resistant).

> *"In the name of the element of fire,*
> *I dedicate you to the divine.*
> *May you provide protection,*
> *evoking positive energy and courage."*

You will now pick up your dish of water. Sprinkle the item with a small amount (or sprinkle water in a circle around it if this is an item that must be kept dry), while saying:

> *"In the name of the element of water,*
> *I dedicate you to the divine.*
> *May you fill my actions with compassion,*
> *giving me the gifts of sight, healing, and dreams."*

Finally, Take a few pinches of soil, sand, or salt, and sprinkle them over the item.

> *"In the name of the element of earth,*
> *I dedicate you to the divine.*
> *May you guide me to respect nature,*
> *supplying wisdom and prosperity to all who are in need."*

Once more, take up your wand, athame, or use your fingers to draw another pentacle over the item.

> *"As above, so below.*
> *I hereby consecrate you in the*
> *name of the Goddess and God.*
> (If you work with individual aspects of the Goddess and God, you can use your deities' names here)
> *So mote it be!"*

This is a very simple and effective ritual for clearing and consecrating. It uses repetitive phrases and sentence structure to make it easier to remember.

You can certainly adapt it to suit your own personal style—some Wiccans, for example, like to cleanse and consecrate their tools by invoking each of the elements, including Akasha—but the steps presented above make a great framework to work with when you're just starting out.

WHEN TO PERFORM THE RITES ON YOUR ITEMS

When it comes to the tools of Wiccan ritual worship—those items that will always be on your altar—it's generally considered essential to perform both steps in the same ritual, more or less like the one provided above.

When it comes to ingredients for spellwork, however, practices tend to vary.

Some Wiccans will do a simpler version of the above ritual.

Others don't feel the need to cast a circle for clearing and charging spellwork ingredients.

Still others will do a basic clearing of the item before the formal ritual work begins, then charge it once in the circle, as part of the spellwork itself. This often depends on the nature and purpose of the spell, the type of object you're clearing and charging, as well as individual preferences.

For example, you might like to charge your crystals in sunlight. Perhaps you'll clear them in the circle and then lay them out to charge the following morning.

As always, follow your intuition when making these decisions. Work in a way that allows you to feel joyful and relaxed about what you're doing.

If you're feeling overwhelmed by the time and effort it takes to clear and charge a dozen items, then you're not likely to put positive energy into them!

CONCLUSION

You now have a basic overview of the purpose of the Wiccan altar and the tools of ritual and spellwork, as well as some common-sense advice for finding, acquiring, and preparing these items for use in your own Wiccan practice.

Although on one level, this guide may seem to cover rather mundane topics, the belief in Wicca is that the divine is in all things because the Goddess and God created everything in our world. There is as much divinity in each of us as there is in the ocean, and as much power in the branch of a tree as in the beam of a temple. Similarly, when we dedicate a physical object like a wand or a chalice to the pursuit of spiritual connection, that's exactly what results.

As you gradually build your own collection of spiritual items, pay attention to how your personal energy feels when interacting with these tools. With time and practice, you will likely find that they become more and more infused with your personal power, and that the quality of focus and energy in ritual and spellwork rises over time.

You will find yourself growing and changing in miraculous ways when you work with the daylight of the God and the moonlight of the Goddess. If you approach your new altar and your new tools with joy and reverence, and are willing to learn and practice, you will learn about your own spiritual power, heal, help others, and help yourself traverse the sometimes-rocky road that's known as life.

Finally, although we've just spent a good deal of energy itemizing the rather long list of tools and other items generally considered to be necessary for Wiccan practice, it's important to stress that nothing at all is *required* for connecting with the Goddess and God beyond your mind, your heart, and your spirit.

Remember that there is no wrong way to practice your faith. Just because one person tells you that you need a particular tool, doesn't make it so. Wicca is all about following your own path, and if you've put off and put off acquiring, say, a robe, it might be your intuition telling you that a particular item is not for you. Perhaps over time your stance will change—that decision is yours to make, though.

On that note, it's time to conclude this book. I hope that this guide has provided you with a solid understanding of the Wicca altar, as well as introducing you to the main tools and supplies of our religion.

It has been an absolute pleasure writing this book, and I hope you have enjoyed reading it.

Thank you one more time for reading.

Blessed Be.

SUGGESTIONS FOR FURTHER READING

While this guide provides a thorough overview of the most commonly used tools for Wiccan ritual and magic, the information here is is by no means the end-all be-all. As you develop your practice, you should feel free to experiment with your approach to ritual and spellwork until you arrive at methods that feel authentic for you.

Reading about these topics—and all aspects of the Craft—is highly recommended. Below is a very brief list of recommended books that can get you started. In these resources, you can find more information about various ways of arranging your altar, more about how tools are used in ritual, different approaches to casting a circle, and much more. You can find these books online and in Wiccan, Pagan, or other "New Age" shops. Happy reading!

Scott Cunningham, *Wicca: A Guide for the Solitary Practitioner* (1989)

Scott Cunningham, *Living Wicca: A Further Guide for the Solitary Practitioner* (1993)

Amaris Silver Moon, *The Essence of Magick: A Wiccan's Guide to Successful Witchcraft* (2015)

Jeanne Mclarney and D.J. Conway, *Wicca: The Complete Craft* (2001)

THREE FREE AUDIOBOOKS PROMOTION

Don't forget, you can now enjoy **three audiobooks completely free of charge** when you start a free 30-day trial with Audible.

If you're new to the Craft, *Wicca Starter Kit* contains three of Lisa's most popular books for beginning Wiccans. You can download it for free at:

www.wiccaliving.com/free-wiccan-audiobooks

Or, if you're wanting to expand your magical skills, check out *Spellbook Starter Kit,* with three collections of spellwork featuring the powerful energies of candles, colors, crystals, mineral stones, and magical herbs. Download over 150 spells for free at:

www.wiccaliving.com/free-spell-audiobooks

Members receive free audiobooks every month, as well as exclusive discounts. And, if you don't want to continue with Audible, just remember to cancel your membership. You won't be charged a cent, and you'll get to keep your books!

Happy listening!

MORE BOOKS BY LISA CHAMBERLAIN

Wicca for Beginners: A Guide to Wiccan Beliefs, Rituals, Magic, and Witchcraft

Wicca Book of Spells: A Book of Shadows for Wiccans, Witches, and Other Practitioners of Magic

Wicca Herbal Magic: A Beginner's Guide to Practicing Wiccan Herbal Magic, with Simple Herb Spells

Wicca Book of Herbal Spells: A Book of Shadows for Wiccans, Witches, and Other Practitioners of Herbal Magic

Wicca Candle Magic: A Beginner's Guide to Practicing Wiccan Candle Magic, with Simple Candle Spells

Wicca Book of Candle Spells: A Book of Shadows for Wiccans, Witches, and Other Practitioners of Candle Magic

Wicca Crystal Magic: A Beginner's Guide to Practicing Wiccan Crystal Magic, with Simple Crystal Spells

Wicca Book of Crystal Spells: A Book of Shadows for Wiccans, Witches, and Other Practitioners of Crystal Magic

Tarot for Beginners: A Guide to Psychic Tarot Reading, Real Tarot Card Meanings, and Simple Tarot Spreads

Runes for Beginners: A Guide to Reading Runes in Divination, Rune Magic, and the Meaning of the Elder Futhark Runes

Wicca Moon Magic: A Wiccan's Guide and Grimoire for Working Magic with Lunar Energies

Wicca Wheel of the Year Magic: A Beginner's Guide to the Sabbats, with History, Symbolism, Celebration Ideas, and Dedicated Sabbat Spells

Wicca Kitchen Witchery: A Beginner's Guide to Magical Cooking, with Simple Spells and Recipes

Wicca Essential Oils Magic: A Beginner's Guide to Working with Magical Oils, with Simple Recipes and Spells

Wicca Elemental Magic: A Guide to the Elements, Witchcraft, and Magical Spells

Wicca Magical Deities: A Guide to the Wiccan God and Goddess, and Choosing a Deity to Work Magic With

Wicca Living a Magical Life: A Guide to Initiation and Navigating Your Journey in the Craft

Magic and the Law of Attraction: A Witch's Guide to the Magic of Intention, Raising Your Frequency, and Building Your Reality

Wicca Altar and Tools: A Beginner's Guide to Wiccan Altars, Tools for Spellwork, and Casting the Circle

Wicca Finding Your Path: A Beginner's Guide to Wiccan Traditions, Solitary Practitioners, Eclectic Witches, Covens, and Circles

Wicca Book of Shadows: A Beginner's Guide to Keeping Your Own Book of Shadows and the History of Grimoires

Modern Witchcraft and Magic for Beginners: A Guide to Traditional and Contemporary Paths, with Magical Techniques for the Beginner Witch

FREE GIFT REMINDER

Just a reminder that Lisa is giving away an exclusive, free spell book as a thank-you gift to new readers!

Little Book of Spells contains ten spells that are ideal for newcomers to the practice of magic, but are also suitable for any level of experience.

Read it on read on your laptop, phone, tablet, Kindle or Nook device by visiting:

<u>www.wiccaliving.com/bonus</u>

DID YOU ENJOY *WICCA ALTAR AND TOOLS*?

Thanks so much for reading this book! I know there are many great books out there about Wicca, so I really appreciate you choosing this one.

If you enjoyed the book, I have a small favor to ask—would you take a couple of minutes to leave a review for this book on Amazon?

Your feedback will help me to make improvements to this book, and to create even better ones in the future. It will also help me develop new ideas for books on other topics that might be of interest to you. Thanks in advance for your help!

Made in the USA
Middletown, DE
17 December 2020